D1151210

B62432

POCKET STUDY SKILLS

Series Editor: **Kate Williams**,
Oxford Brookes University, UK

For the time-pushed student, the *Pocket Study Skills* pack a lot of advice into a little book. Each guide focuses on a single crucial aspect of study giving you step-by-step guidance, handy tips and clear advice on how to approach the important areas which will continually be at the core of your study ethic.

Published

Blogs, Wikis, Podcasts and More   *Andy Pulman*
Brilliant Writing Tips for Students   *Julia Copus*
Getting Critical   *Kate Williams*
Planning Your Essay   *Janet Godwin*
Referencing and Understanding Plagiarism
   Kate Williams and Jude Carroll
Science Study Skills   *Sue Robbins*

Further titles are planned

Pocket Study Skills

Series Standing Order
ISBN 978-0230-21605-1
(outside North America only)

You can receive future titles in this series as they are published by placing a standing order. Please contact your bookseller or, in case of difficulty, write to us at the address below with your name and address, the title of the series and the ISBN quoted above.

Customer Services Department,
Macmillan Distribution Ltd
Houndmills, Basingstoke, Hampshire
RG21 6XS England

SCIENCE STUDY SKILLS

POCKET STUDY SKILLS

Sue Robbins

palgrave
macmillan

Palgrave Macmillan in the UK is an imprint of Macmillan Publishers Limited, registered in England, company number 785998, of 4 Crinan Street, London, N1 9XW

Palgrave® and Macmillan® are registered trademarks in the United States, the United Kingdom, Europe and other countries

ISBN-13: 978-0-230-57763-3

This book is printed on paper suitable for recycling and made from fully managed and sustained forest sources. Logging, pulping and manufacturing processes are expected to conform to the environmental regulations of the country of origin.

A catalogue record for this book is available from the British Library.

First published 2009 by PALGRAVE MACMILLAN

Printed and bound by CPI Group (UK) Ltd, Croydon, CR0 4YY

Contents

Acknowledgements

Thanks are due to my students who over the past two decades have inspired me in my teaching and challenged me to explain scientific process and conventions of scientific writing. This little book is written for their successors. I have written it as if they were in the room with me and I was explaining each topic to them face to face. I hope, therefore, that they find it easy to read and understand!

Kate Williams is the person who first got me thinking about communicating study skills to science students. We have worked together for 13 years, bouncing ideas off each other and putting together materials to help science students with their assignments. Thank you, Kate, for the hours spent pouring over scripts and cappuccinos!

My colleague Andrew Rendell works with me in Life Sciences. He has helped develop materials for our students and provided me with welcome back-up and support as I have rolled out the delivery of study skills to our science students. Thank you, Andrew.

Finally, I would like to thank Sallie Godwin for her delightful illustrations.

1 Doing science

Science is a practical discipline; it's hands-on. Being a scientist is not a spectator sport. It's about *you* finding out: *you* observing, *you* recording, *you* attending to detail, *you* being honest about *your* findings. Then it's about interpreting what *you*'ve observed. It's about asking questions like, 'How?', 'Why?' and seeking the answers. It's not about making predictions, then looking for evidence to support your ideas.

To do this you must refer to the body of knowledge that we already have, so you're standing on the shoulders of scientists who have gone before you as you reach for the sky. This means that you read textbooks to get the overall picture and learn the language of science, which has differing dialects for the different disciplines. Then, as you become more knowledgeable and specialised in a particular area, you will need to probe deeply into current thinking, searching through journals for academic papers because that is how front-line scientists publish their work.

What types of coursework are you likely to be asked to produce?

These are the kinds of work you will be expected to do:

- lab and/or field notebooks/diaries
- lab and/or field reports
- essays: scientific, academic
- posters: scientific, academic
- problem solving: numerical, statistical, data handling.

You will also be required to sit exams where you will need to produce essays, solve problems, handle data and answer multiple choice questions (MCQs) under time constraints.

This guide is designed (i) to help you understand your lecturers' expectations of you as a science student and (ii) to provide you with step-by-step guidance as you study and prepare work for assessment. I hope that you will be excited by the discoveries you make as you study science and that this little book will help and encourage you to become fully involved and get the most out of your degree.

The secret to success is PLANNING: organising your time.

Term/semester planning

It is a good idea to plan your study time for the term/semester:

▶ Draw up a plan of the whole term or semester (see sample timetable on next page).

▶ Now put in your coursework deadlines and exam dates for each module or unit – the fixed points.

▶ Next, write down when you will start each piece of work. For this you will need to decide how much time you need to prepare the work.

Degree-level coursework can seldom be knocked up in one evening!

Planning the term/semester: First, note the deadlines; then work backwards to plan your work.

Week	Module/ subject name	Module/ subject name	Module/ subject name	Module/ subject name	Module/ subject name
1					
2					
3					
4					
5					
6					
7					
8					
9					
10					
11					
12					

Why will you do practical work?

Lab and fieldwork classes are designed to support your learning. Often they will demonstrate the principles that you have covered in lectures. In most universities these classes are compulsory because as scientists we are keen that you participate actively in 'doing science'. Practical work is the fun part where you are finding things out for yourself.

How can you get the most out of your practical class?

You'll get the most out of your practical class if you plan and prepare for your class beforehand.

Normally you will have access to the practical schedule before your lab or field session. If so, be certain to:

- Read it through carefully and make sure that you understand what the work is about.
- Look up references if you have been given them – read around the subject area in your textbook and/or lecture notes.
- Think through the method and make sure that you can follow it easily.
- Try to visualise what you will be doing. If you have to prepare samples, think through the process and the skills you will need. Think as a scientist!

Recording science: lab diaries

Science is written down as we do it. We don't rely on remembering what we did, measurements we made and results we obtained. That would be too risky: it wouldn't be accurate. To avoid muddling ourselves and our work, we record everything we do in the laboratory in a diary or notebook *while we are doing it*. This forms a permanent record of our time in the lab. It's a blow-by-blow account of what we did, what we saw and what we found. You do not rewrite your lab diary afterwards; it must remain authentic.

There are particular conventions that we have to follow with regard to writing up and recording information.

A lab diary is a bound book with pages numbered, work dated, written in pen (not water-soluble ink), mistakes crossed out but not erased. Having said all that, you are free to record your work in a personal way and without writing full sentences, e.g.: '*I mixed the 3 solutions – see schedule p4 section 2(a) – then I put the test tube in the 37 °C waterbath to incubate for 20 minutes. Timed it with my stop-clock.*'

It is organised under headings:

Title: Should be brief but accurately describe the experiment or activity.

Introduction: Why you are doing the work, providing the context and reason.

Aim: What you set out to do: be concise (= few words) and precise (= accurate).

Method: How you did it. If you have been given a practical schedule containing the method, then refer to it; don't copy it out again. Do note down any points where you departed from your written instructions. For an experiment of your own design, write out your method in full.

Observations/results: What you saw and measurements you made, all put into tables (see examples). Do not fabricate any results.

Data handling: Any graphs, working out of data etc.; evidence for your conclusions.

Conclusions: What you found out – nothing more, nothing less! If your work was inconclusive, say so; there's no disgrace in that!

Data handling and drawing conclusions usually happens after you have left the lab, although there are occasions when you will hand-plot a graph so that you can decide whether you have collected sufficient data, or whether you need to extend your sample range.

Date of work *Place of work*

17/09/08   Lab: S310   — *Who you worked with*

Lab Partner: K. Smith

Demonstrator: Dr. Jones   — *Who taught you*

Salting out haemoglobin: — *Title*
Determining the solubility
of haemoglobin in
ammonium sulfate solution.

Introduction: This is crude
method for separating proteins

Aim: To find out the
concentration of ammonium
sulfate needed to precipitate
haemoglobin from a solution
containing a mixture of proteins.

Method: Abbreviations:
Hb = haemoglobin
$(NH_4)_2SO_4$ = ammonium sulfate

Follow the method as   — *Refer to any prac. manual rather than copy it out*
given in the practical
booklet by Dr. Jones.
(see pages 5-8).

Pipetting schedule:

Tube No.	Vol $(NH_4)_2SO_4$ (mL)	Vol H_2O (mL)	$(NH_4)_2SO_4$ % saturation
1	0.0	10.0	0
2	6.0	4.0	60
3	6.5	3.5	65
4	7.0	3.0	70
5	7.5	2.5	75
6	8.0	2.0	80

Next ...

Observations: — *Write down any unusual things that you noticed*

1. Hb solution was very
thick which made it
difficult to pipette into
the test tubes.

2. $(NH_4)_2SO_4$ solution has
crystals in the bathroom
of the jar, showing that
it is a saturated solution.

Figure 1: Example of lab diary

Recording science: field notebooks

In some areas of science practical work takes place not in the lab, but out in the field. This is particularly the case for environment disciplines. Recording science outdoors presents its own challenges. The weather can be foul, the fieldwork can be aquatic (intentionally or unintentionally!) and a traditional lab diary would disintegrate after a short period of exposure to the elements. So field notebooks are made of waterproof paper and you write on this paper using a pencil rather than a pen. It still must be a permanent record of your time in the field, so put a line through any errors, don't erase them. Have elastic bands to hold the pages down in the open-book position, otherwise the wind might rip them out!

Apart from all that, field notebooks serve the same function and observe the same rules as lab diaries. They are set out in a similar way, particularly using grids of various kinds to log samples and track numbers of observations.

SNAILS
DAY①

Drawing tables

The clearest way of recording experimental data is in tables.

- Draw a table in your lab diary or field notebook *before* you start collecting your data.
- Give a heading to each column that describes what the numbers or observations refer to.
- Put in the correct units for numerical data. Now you can enter your data without units since these are in the column heading.

Use tables in your method if you are making up a series of samples using repetitive techniques such as pipetting solutions. This can help reduce errors.

The next few pages use **an example of a real lab practical** to show you how to set out your work and record your results.

Here are the instructions given in your practical schedule or script:

Title: Salting out haemoglobin: Determining the solubility of haemoglobin in ammonium sulfate solution.

Aim: To find out the concentration of ammonium sulfate needed to precipitate haemoglobin from a solution containing a mixture of proteins.

Introduction: Proteins vary in their solubility in salt solutions due to their differences in amino acid content … 'Salting out' refers to the process of precipitating proteins from solutions as solids. It results in a crude extract and this method is often the first step in the preparation of pure protein extracts. The most common salt used to precipitate proteins is ammonium sulfate.

Method: Set up 6 test tubes containing the following percentages of ammonium sulfate: 0, 60, 65, 70, 75, 80%.

Now you can see how the lab diary in Figure 1 follows this structure. The title and aims have been taken directly from the schedule, but the introduction is just a one-line summary.

Next we come to the *Method*. In your lab diary you need to work out how you will produce samples of 0, 60, 65, 70, 75, 80% ammonium sulfate.

Table 1 is a useful table to help you with making up your samples: work this out before your lab class and put it in your method; you will find it makes life easier for you in the lab. Draw a grid in your lab diary:

Table 1: Volumes of reagents to be pipetted into test tubes to make up samples 1–6

1	2	3	4
Tube No.	Vol $(NH_4)_2SO_4$ (mL)	Vol H_2O (mL)	$(NH_4)_2SO_4$ (% saturation)
1	0.0	10.0	0
2	6.0	4.0	60
3	6.5	3.5	65
4	7.0	3.0	70
5	7.5	2.5	75
6	8.0	2.0	80

Column 1: number your samples (for easy reference).

Columns 2 and 3: headings give the reagent (chemical substance, e.g., water, ammonium sulfate) + units of volume, so you only need to put numbers showing quantities against each sample.

Column 4: shows the concentration of reagent in each sample.

Note this convention: headings for tables go *above* the table. Think 'table cloth': a table cloth sits on top of a table. ────

You can see that Table 1 was used in the lab diary example (Figure 1).

The next step in this practical is to add 1 mL of haemoglobin solution to each tube, mix well, allow to stand for 15 minutes, then filter off the precipitate. The absorbance of the filtrate is then read in the spectrophotometer at a wavelength (λ) of 578 nm.

Table 2 is the results table:

Table 2: Absorbance measurements for samples 1–6 and calculation of % haemoglobin left in solution

Note the jump in ammonium sulfate concentration between tubes 1 and 2. There is a 60% change, whereas the difference between tubes 2 and 3, 3 and 4, 4 and 5, 5 and 6 is only 5%. This gives you a non-linear increase in salt concentration.

1	4	5	6
Tube no.	$(NH_4)_2SO_4$ (%)	Absorbance at λ 578 nm	Haemoglobin (%)
1	0	1.250	100
2	60	1.200	96
3	65	1.063	85
4	70	0.750	60
5	75	0.350	28
6	80	0.063	5

Columns 1 and 4: from Table 1.

Column 5: readings from the spectrophotometer. Absorbance has no units, but put in the wavelength that you used.

Column 6: taking tube 1 as 100% haemoglobin, calculations of % haemoglobin for samples 2–6.

The results from Table 2 can now be used to draw a graph to determine the percentage saturation of ammonium sulfate needed to precipitate the bulk of haemoglobin in a solution.

Drawing graphs

Graphs are another way of recording experimental data.

1 Decide what you want to plot.
2 Choose appropriate scales.
3 X axis (horizontal): the quantity that you can control.
4 Y axis (vertical): the quantity that you measured, the variable.
5 Label both axes and take care to put in the correct *units*.
6 Give your graph a title, but do not put 'A graph to show …': we can see it is a graph! Just state what it *does* show – and put the title underneath.

So, with our example, the instruction you have been given is: 'Using the data from Table 2, plot column 6 against column 4'. What does this mean?

▸ 'Against column 4' means that column 4 is the variable that you had control over. These are the concentrations of ammonium sulfate that you set. You plot these on the horizontal axis, the X axis.

- Column 6 is the quantity that you have calculated from the absorbance readings in column 5. (You had no control over the readings in column 5. They were your results.) You plot these on the vertical axis, the Y axis:

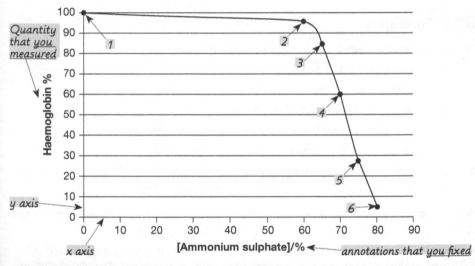

Figure 2: Salting out of haemoglobin: % haemoglobin left in solution at various saturation levels of ammonium sulfate.

Note this convention: A figure is any kind of illustration that isn't a table. Graphs, charts (pie charts, bar charts, etc.), pictures, diagrams, the insert from a lab diary shown in this book are all figures.

Headings or titles for figures go *below* the figure. A graph is a figure. Think: 'a figure needs something to stand on'.

Interpretation of Figure 2

Now that you have represented your results as a graph you are in a position to interpret the data.

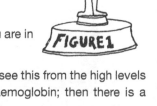

Haemoglobin remains in solution in samples 1–3. You can see this from the high levels in Figure 2. Sample 4 shows a slightly lower level of haemoglobin; then there is a dramatic drop in levels in samples 5 and 6.

This means that haemoglobin remains in solution until ammonium sulfate saturation reaches about 70%. Increasing the saturation of ammonium sulfate beyond 70% causes haemoglobin to come out of solution and form a precipitate. In the method the precipitate was filtered off and the absorbance of the filtrate recorded, so for samples 5 and 6 the haemoglobin has precipitated out, been filtered off and therefore the absorbance of the filtrate is very low.

Here is an example of an incorrectly drawn graph for this data. What is wrong with this graph?

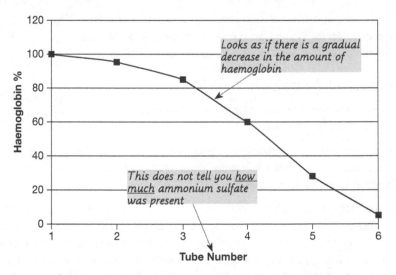

Figure 3: Salting out of haemoglobin: % haemoglobin left in solution for tubes 1–6 (an incorrect graph).

Plotting tube number against haemoglobin % spaces the points out equally from each other along the X axis. However, earlier on we noted that in our experiment we did not use an even distribution of ammonium sulphate across the tubes. We saw that there was a 60% difference between tubes 1 and 2, but only 5% between each other consecutive tube. So Figure 3 does not accurately represent the data that we collected; even worse, it leads to errors in interpretation.

It is worth noting that you would get the same-shaped graph if you foreshortened the scale on the X axis for Figure 3, making the points 0, 60, 65, 70, 75, 80% equally spaced apart (not acknowledging that 0–60 is *not* the same as 60–65, 65–70 etc.).

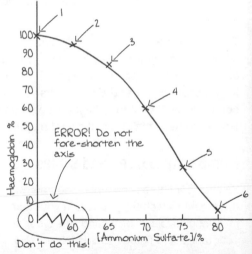

Figure 4: Salting out of haemoglobin: % haemoglobin left in solution at various saturation levels of ammonium sulfate.

Interpretation of Figure 3 (the incorrect graph)

Here we do not see the dramatic drop-off in haemoglobin solubility. It looks as if there is an almost proportional relationship between the amount of haemoglobin remaining in solution with tube number and hence ammonium sulphate concentration. Because we have not acknowledged the 0%–60% change in ammonium sulphate concentration between tubes 1 and 2, we cannot correctly interpret the effect of ammonium sulphate on haemoglobin solubility.

Take-home message: *Be really careful that you represent your data appropriately when drawing graphs. Think before you draw*: Am I plotting these points correctly, accurately, using appropriate scales? This is particularly something that you need to think about when using Excel to draw your graphs. *You* must do the thinking. Your computer can't do it for you. It will come up with a default graph but it's your responsibility to check that it is in the right mode!

Numbering figures and tables

You number figures and tables separately in the order in which they appear in your text. In a longish piece of writing the order of your tables and figures could look like this:

Table 1 ~~~~~~~~
Figure 1 ~~~~~~~~
Figure 2 ~~~~~~~~
Figure 3 ~~~~~~~~
Table 2 ~~~~~~~~

The secret to success is PLANNING: organising your time.

Week-by-week planning

It is a good idea to plan your study time within each week:

▶ Draw up a plan for the week (see sample timetable on next page).
▶ Put in your lecture/tutorial/laboratory times.
▶ Put in your paid employment times.
▶ Now put in study times.

Give yourself time to play sport and have a social life, so …

▶ Put in times for sport, clubs, or other social events.

Being a student should be fun: neither all work and no play, nor all play and no work!
Planning your time should help you get the balance right and meet your deadlines.

Planning the week: For each day insert activities for morning, afternoon and evening.

Monday	Tuesday	Wednesday	Thursday	Friday	Saturday	Sunday
Chemistry lecture	Chemistry practical		Biology practical	Maths tutorial	Paid work	
	Biology lecture	Play hockey				Visit parents
Paid work		Socialise		Paid work	Socialise	

As you carried out your experiment you *wrote down* what you were doing in your lab diary or field notebook. Provided you set out your work clearly so that it can be understood, you can use any writing style that you think appropriate.

Next we will think about *writing up* your experiment. This is where you use your blow-by-blow account to write a scientific report, so the quality of your initial recording will affect the quality and ease with which you can write your final report.

A report is a formal piece of writing and there are conventions that you must follow:

- Write in the past tense – this is especially important for your methods section since you are reporting work you have already done.
- Don't use personal pronouns: 'I put the test tube in the 37 °C water bath to incubate for 20 minutes'; instead use the passive tense: 'The test tube was placed in the 37 °C water bath …' Your reader is interested in what was done but not in who personally did it.

Report structure

Follow the headings listed below:

Title; Introduction; Aim; Method:
(refer to 'Recording science: lab diaries' in Chapter 1).

Results: Worked data either as tables or as graphs. Do not put in raw data (as collected in the lab) – these go in the Appendix – but show the final version of your results after you have done your calculations. Only represent a set of data once, i.e., don't put in a table and a graph for the same data. Put the graph in the results and the table in the Appendix.

Discussion: Here you need to have thought through what your data mean. Don't make sweeping statements that go beyond what you have observed. Do put your results in context by reading around the published literature and referencing anything that you use in your argument.

Conclusions: Succinctly pull together the main points from your discussion. Don't present any new evidence or refer to any further published work in this section.

References: List the references cited in your report in the way that your module handbook says. Here we use Harvard style, which is commonly used in science.

Appendix: Tables of raw data, calculations used to produce worked data.

The diagram overleaf illustrates the interrelationships between the different sections of a scientific report. Note that *everything* relates back to the **Aims**; therefore it is vital that you spend time working these out carefully. Aims need to be focused and specific. Try to write your aims as a question that you want to answer. The rest of the report tells the story of how you tackled that question and went about answering it (your **Method**).

At the end, your **Discussion** will look back at how far the **Results** you obtained helped you to answer the question that you set in your **Aims**, and your **Conclusion** will summarise your findings.

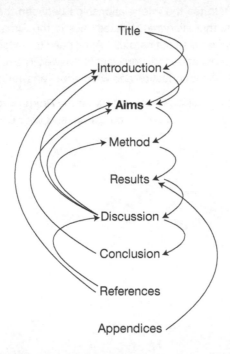

Title

Introduction

Aims

Method

Results

Discussion

Conclusion

References

Appendices

Writing scientific reports

Use formal language. Write in the past tense with attention to grammar and spelling. Don't use personal pronouns ('I' or 'we'). The reader is interested in what happened, not who did it!

Title: This should be brief, factual and specific. Relate this to Aims.

Abstract: This is a summary and should include a brief introduction to the topic, the main points of the method, the main points of the results and the principal conclusions. Write this last.

Introduction: This sets the scene. Here you provide background information from your reading (referenced), providing the context for your investigation (why you did it).

Aims: This is the question that you wanted to answer. Write a brief statement about the experiment. Clearly and concisely tell the reader what you were trying to do.

Materials and methods: Here you record what was actually done in the experiment – how it was carried out. You may have modified a method given you in your practical booklet; if so, you must write these changes down. This is an account of how the experiment was set up, what the treatments were, what controls were used, how many replicates per treatment, etc. There should be enough detail that the reader could repeat your experiment purely on the basis of your report and without discussing it with you. *Do make sure* this correlates accurately with your lab diary or field notebook.

Results: Present a concise summary of your results in words, referring to any graphs and/or diagrams that you have used by their appropriate figure or table number.

▶ Figures and tables should appear in the text as soon as possible after their first mention in the text. Remember: Table titles go above the table; figure titles go below the figure.

▶ Do not present the same data in more than one way. Choose the clearest way of presenting it.

▶ Raw data should be placed in an appendix at the end of the report.

Discussion: *This is where you interpret your results.* Try to explain them and relate them to one another and put them into the context of your reading of previously published work, relating them to your introduction.

Go no further than the experiment shows. Refer back to the Aims and the Introduction and discuss your results in relation to points made there.

Critically assess the methods you used. Think about how well

FIGURE 1

your practical work went and what lessons you have learned about your lab technique from doing this experiment. Would you recommend changes to the design of the experiment?

You can only make definite statements about the outcome of your experiment if adequate controls were used. You should only alter one part of your experiment at a time, keeping everything else constant (e.g., when looking at an enzyme's rate of reaction, keep a constant pH, enzyme concentration and temperature but change the substrate concentration). If you do that, then it is easier to interpret any changes you find because they will result from the alteration that you made to the conditions of your experiment.

Conclusions: Pull the whole report together in a concluding paragraph that relates back to your Aims. Do not bring in new evidence here. It may be that nothing conclusive can be seen from your experiment, or that the experiment needs refining for repeating in the future. Don't make wide sweeping statements or assumptions that can't be backed up by your data. This is where reviewing ('how I'd do it differently next time') comes in.

References: Harvard style is used in this guide and widely used in science (see p. 43).

Appendix: Raw data, calculations.

Numbering systems and subheadings

In a long written report a numbering system can help your reader to navigate your report.

Here is an example:

Title: Study of the distribution of the dragonfly *Anax imperator* along the margins of the River Thames within the city boundaries of Oxford.

Abstract: Amid concerns that the habitat of *Anax imperator* was being adversely affected by boating on the Thames, a survey of the riverbanks was conducted and the main populations of this dragonfly identified. The method used to count the population … and results showed …

---

1 Introduction

Anax imperator is a member of the Aeshnidae family of dragonflies and can frequently be seen darting among the rushes alongside riverbanks. It is blue in colour and in common with all dragonflies, has two pairs of wings …

2 Aims

2.1 To identify whether *Anax imperator* is found in all locations along the Thames or whether there are particular habitats …

2.2 To determine whether *Anax imperator* is affected by human disturbance due to …

3 Materials and methods

3.1 Sampling was carried out at 50 metre intervals along a 3 km stretch …

3.2 Data analysis was carried out …

3.3 Disturbance of habitat was measured by …

3.4 The method published by Jones et al. (2006) provided …

4 Results

4.1 *Identification of species and location of habitat*: Figure 1 shows the distribution of *Anax imperator* across the study area …

4.2 *Measurement of disturbance*: Evidence from … showed that … and so on.

What is a deadline?

A deadline is the FINAL time that work will be accepted. Work will be accepted *up to* the deadline, not beyond (without penalty).

What a deadline is *not* ...

▶ A deadline is *not* a target time that you aim for and hope you meet.

▶ A deadline is *not* flexible. If you miss it, you will receive a penalty.

▶ It's like going to catch a train. If your train leaves at 09.05 then you will not expect it to be waiting for you if you turn up at 09.20 or even 09.10! If you are serious about catching the 09.05 train then you will make sure you're at the station by 09.00 at the latest.

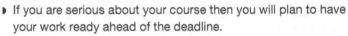

▶ If you are serious about your course then you will plan to have your work ready ahead of the deadline.

You are expected to read round your lecture subjects and read for assignments, so it's important that you have an up-to-date textbook and are able to read effectively. Reading science textbooks and scientific papers is a skill in itself.

Consolidating your lecture notes

Lectures provide the framework for your personal study; they are not an end in themselves. You will be expected to read around the subject covered in each lecture. Handouts from lectures are a useful starting point but you should supplement them with your own notes if you are to gain the most from your lectures. You will need good notes to aid your revision at exam time. So how do you do this?

Tips for making good lecture notes

1 Attend all lectures and make sure that you get any handouts on offer.
2 Make notes in lectures to supplement handouts.
3 Note down references that are recommended.
4 After the lecture, within 24 hours, go through your notes and make sure that they are
   (a) legible, (b) logical and (c) complete.

If you do rewrite your notes, don't throw away the originals – they may jog your memory during exam revision. You may be able to picture that part of the lecture from your notes and find it helpful.

Supplementing your notes

As you re-read your lecture notes, go to the relevant sections in your textbook and:

1 Select a section of 2–3 pages and read it without writing anything down.
2 Shut your book and make notes of the key points.
3 Next, re-read the textbook passage and see whether you've missed any major points. If you have, jot them down.
4 Write down the reference so that you can look it up when you come to revise.

Use this method for supplementing lecture notes and when researching for an essay or other coursework. A major benefit is that you have made notes from your textbook using your own words (because the book was closed), so there is little danger of plagiarism.

Making notes from academic papers

As you progress with your studies you will be expected to read original scientific papers rather than just the digested forms in textbooks. This will allow you to make your own judgements about the claims of the author(s) and appropriateness of the conclusions.

Academic papers begin with an *Abstract*. This is a summary of the paper's contents and is really useful in helping you to decide whether the paper is relevant to your needs.

Unless you are wanting to replicate experimental work, you can probably get away with reading the:

▶ *Introduction*: context of the work carried out; literature review, you should be able to pick up on other useful references from this.
▶ *Results*: worked data from the experiments.
▶ *Discussion*: relating the Results to previously published work in the field as outlined in the Introduction.
▶ *Conclusions*: summary of findings and pointing to the next area for research.

Skimming through the *Method* is useful, but details of *Materials* are often not necessary.

Having read the paper, you are now in a position to make notes of the relevant parts. Read through one section, close the paper and write a brief summary. Now go on to the next section and do the same. Again, by summarising without looking at the paper you will be using your own words, thus reducing the risk of plagiarism.

Remember to write down the Harvard reference for the paper. You'll need that when you use your notes in your own work. See next section: 'Essays in science'.

By reading a selection of original papers on a topic of interest you will begin to get a feel for the world of scientific research. Scientific papers are models for your own writing as a scientist.

Three key differences between studying at school and university

1 No one will chase you if you don't show up for lectures.
2 No one will chase you if you don't hand in your coursework.
3 No one will manage your time for you.

You are expected to manage your time in a responsible way and to plan to meet your deadlines – more of that later …

Other differences:

▸ If you want to eat then you'll need time to go shopping and to cook your meals.
▸ If you want clean clothes (and we'd like that) then you need time to do your washing (and even your ironing!).
▸ You will need to manage your money, rent, communal living.

So, on a day-to-day basis you will need to juggle various different time commitments and decide on your own priorities, e.g., study, paid employment, family responsibilities, your social life, etc.

4   Essays in science

'I've got to write an essay about haemoglobin [or earthworms, or volt meters, or anionic surfactants, or anything else] and I don't know where to begin …'

So where do you begin when you are set an essay in science? As Dylan Thomas said in *Under Milk Wood*: 'To begin at the beginning …'

That sounds like a good place to start, so … What *really* is the subject of your essay? It is unlikely to be everything about haemoglobin (or earthworms, or volt meters, or anionic surfactants, or anything else). You will be required to be discriminating, choosing only what is necessary to answer the question and complete the task set, so read the title carefully.

What's in a title?

What are you being asked to do? You need to study the title: Is it a question? What are the 'instruction' words? Instructions tell you what type of essay it is and how to tackle the question set. There are two basic kinds:

1 *Descriptive*: These may have the following words in the title: 'demonstrate', 'describe', 'identify', 'outline', 'explain', 'summarise'.
2 *Present an argument*: Typical words and phrases here are: 'compare and contrast', 'discuss', 'evaluate', 'examine the evidence', 'what is the evidence for ...', 'argue a case', 'to what extent ...?'

You may find that you have a mix of both types, forming a two-part essay, for example: *Outline the factors currently thought to contribute to global warming. How convincing is the evidence that reducing carbon emissions from vehicles will have any effect on levels of greenhouse gases?*

So, first of all you must decide what type of essay you have been set, since that will dictate the style of essay you research and write. See *Planning Your Essay* in this series.

Looking for information

Having decided what you need to research, you need to look for good sources of information. This is an academic piece of work so you need to use academically sound sources. If you want a view on the news, you read about it in the newspaper. If you want to answer a science question you don't go to the newspaper; instead you go to places where science is published: the scientific literature. Science stories in newspapers represent the opinions of the journalists who wrote them and may well be scientifically inaccurate. You must use sources backed up by evidence.

For definitions, start with your textbook or a scientific dictionary. You can use Wikipedia, but remember this is *not* a peer-reviewed source – anyone can add to it. However, it is a quick way to look up definitions and gives you a starting point.

For content, you will use your textbooks, scientific journal papers, Google Scholar. You need peer-reviewed journals, i.e., ones that have been vetted for quality by scientists working in the same field of study.

Leaving your tracks

You need to **track the process** by which you pull your essay together. This is vital for academic rigor, so keep a notebook or folder in which you write down all your sources, the references you have used, how they were useful, what you learned from them.

For web sources it's a good idea to print off at least the first page, since these resources change from day to day.

What we want to see is **evidence** backing up your statements, **a trail of your footprints** through the literature. Each step is a **reference** with a few words about how it contributes to your understanding.

So … **keep records of the sources** you use (everything you read) and, for each one, make notes in your own words. You also need to write the full reference and make a list of all your sources. Your university may give you access to computer software that can help you with this. Ask your librarian.

Referencing and quoting in science

One of the biggest issues faced by university staff is deciding whether students have submitted their own work or that of somebody else.

Plagiarism is the technical name given to the form of cheating where you try to pass off someone else's work as your own. This may not be a deliberate act; it can be very subtle. It will arise if you don't acknowledge your sources in your work by providing references to show where the information you use has come from.

Quoting: In science we don't quote sources verbatim. What does this mean? Don't lift sentences, paragraphs, straight from a source, put them in speech marks ('…') and give a reference. That may be acceptable in non-science subjects but not in science. Scientists use their own words to summarise key findings when writing from a source. You will be expected to understand what you read and use the ideas in your essay, putting them in context in your own words and acknowledging where the ideas came from, with references, of course. Only on very rare occasions would a scientist use a quotation, such as when referring to a well-known Nobel laureate who had made a famous remark (Crick and Watson's 'double helix', for example).

Harvard referencing system

In science a very common method for referencing is the **Harvard system**. There are two parts to referencing:

1 *Citing your source in the text*: Show where you have used the reference in your writing. For occasions where you use the author's name in the sentence:
   ▶ one author: surname only, then year of publication in brackets: Jones (2008)
   ▶ two authors: Smith and Jones (2007)
   ▶ more than two authors: Brown et al. (2006).

   Where you refer to an idea but without the author's name in the sentence, cite their work as soon as possible after you have written the idea, giving the name(s) and year of publication all in brackets: (Jones 2008); (Smith and Jones 2007); (Brown et al. 2006). You acknowledge your sources in your writing in a shortened version at the point that you used them.

2 *Reference list*: You provide a complete reference list at the end of your work where you give the full details of your sources so that your reader can look them up for themselves. They may want to do further research and your references will provide a suitable starting point.

Details for your reference list

Refer to *Referencing and Understanding Plagiarism* in this series for standard layout and more detail.

Journals

1 Author(s). For each author: surname followed by initials.
2 Year of publication (in brackets).
3 Title of the paper.
4 Title of the journal: shortened version, *in italics*, or <u>underlined</u>, or **bold**.
5 Volume and issue number of the journal.
6 Pages in the journal where the paper is written.

Example: Davis, A.M. (2005) A Breath of Solar Air. *Nature* 434, 577–578.

Books

1 Author(s). For each author: surname followed by initials.
2 Year of publication (in brackets).
3 Title of the book, *in italics*, with main words starting with capital letters.
4 Title of the series and volume number (if one of a series).
5 The edition, if not the first edition.
6 Place of publication and publisher, separated by a colon (:).

Example: Sadava, D., Heller, H.C., Orians, G.H., Purves, W.K., Hillis, D.M. (2008). *Life, the Science of Biology*. 8th edition. Gordonsville: Freeman.

If it is an **online book**:

Example: Sadava, D., Heller, H.C., Orians, G.H., Purves, W.K., Hillis, D.M. (2008). Life, the Science of Biology. 8th edition. Freeman. Retrieved on 27 March 2008 from http://www.whfreeman.com/thelifewirebridge2/

Web sources

1 Sponsor of the website (this is the author).
2 Year of publication (in brackets).
3 Title of the article.
4 'Available at'.
5 The full web address path, followed by the date you visited the website.

Example: Dept of Health (2008) New doctors to help problem drinkers. Available at http://www.dh.gov.uk/en/News/Recentstories/DH_083567 (Accessed 27 March 2008)

When to use a bibliography

A bibliography is a list of sources that you have read but not cited. Often this will be your background reading in preparation for tackling your essay. Commonly it's reading from core textbooks that you need to do before you are able to understand the more specialised literature. The information you gained from this reading will be the more well-known or standard science that you needed to grasp before launching into the focused publications that make up your reference list.

For the essay examples given earlier:
Haemoglobin: you would need to read about haemoglobin structure and oxy-deoxy states before tackling the advanced biochemistry.
Earthworms: you would read about their anatomy and physiology, preferred environment etc.
Volt meters: you need a background understanding of electrical circuits, or physics.
Anionic surfactants: you would make sure you understand what is meant by a surfactant and the background chemistry.

Formatting a bibliography

Use the same formatting as for your Harvard reference list.

Essay plan

Having done your research, you are now ready to plan out your essay. There are many different ways of planning essays. Here are a couple of ideas:

1 **Brainstorm** all the points you need to cover in order to write your essay, checking that you have addressed the question asked, not the one you wish they'd asked!
   - Next, group the ideas into topics. These will become your paragraphs.
   - Starting with the first topic, number the points in the order that you want them in your essay.
   - Go on to the next topic and continue numbering your points.
   - And so on …

2 **Mind maps** are a pictorial method for laying out your plan:
   - Write your title in the middle of a page like the hub of a wheel.
   - Draw balloons all round the hub, with strings like spokes to the centre.
   - Write each idea in a separate balloon. You may need branches from the balloons, showing subsections of an idea.
   - Now group your ideas into topics, using coloured highlighters to mark the groups.
   - Number the topics in the order that you will introduce them, so that the subject matter flows in a logical order from one topic to the next.
   - Number the ideas in each group in the order that you want them in your essay.

An example of how to tackle an essay question

How is the concentration of glucose in the bloodstream kept relatively constant for an athlete playing a 90-minute game of football?

First, read the question carefully and decide what it's about:

1 **Topic**: Regulation of blood glucose levels during exercise. Need to think about *why* blood glucose needs to be kept stable, what it's used for, demands of exercising skeletal muscle. Having analysed the question, the next step is to …

2 **Brainstorm**: blood sugar levels; insulin; glucagon; glucose; liver regulating glucose levels; pancreas; skeletal muscle energy needs for contraction; stability and stress; glucose as energy source; glycogen as glucose store; lactic acid; ATP as energy currency of cells; Cori cycle; carbon cycling; oxidation of glucose to carbon dioxide and water.

3 **Number and group the items**: (1) Stability and stress; (2) skeletal muscle needs energy for contraction; (3) ATP as energy currency of cells; (4) glucose as energy source; (5) insulin, glucagon and pancreas; (6) blood sugar levels; (7) liver regulating glucose levels; (8) glycogen as glucose store; (9) oxidation of glucose to carbon dioxide and water; (10) lactic acid; (11) Cori cycle, carbon cycling.

See the mind map opposite, which shows the same thinking in a different layout.

Mind Map

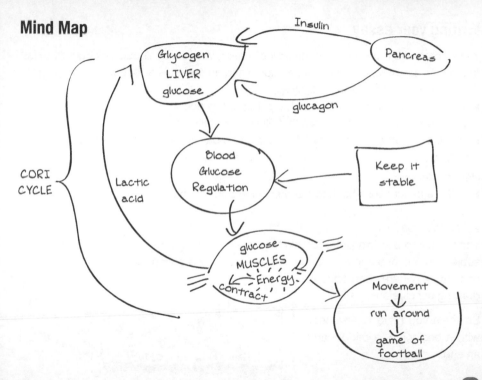

Writing your essay

You've prepared thoroughly, so the task of writing your essay should not daunt you (as much!). An essay has a beginning, a middle and an end. It is arranged in **paragraphs**. Structure your paragraphs as follows:

▶ *topic sentence*: introduces what the paragraph is about
▶ *explanation of topic*: sentences that fill in the details
▶ *concluding sentence*: rounds off the topic and paves the way for the next paragraph.

Next paragraph:

▶ *topic sentence*: links back to the preceding paragraph and introduces the next idea

   …

▶ … and so on

The first paragraph is an introduction to your essay topic, providing the context of your subject. The final paragraph rounds off the essay by drawing together your argument and, only where appropriate, drawing conclusions.

So there you have it, an essay with a beginning, a middle and an end!

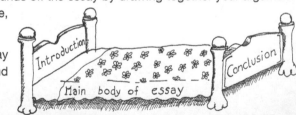

Structuring your essay

The ideas or topics that you've identified will form the paragraphs of your essay. Having decided the order in which you will cover each topic, you now have no worries about what to write next. It's all set down, so you can concentrate on what you are writing without panicking about what follows next (or doesn't!).

First, though, you need an **introduction**. This sets the scene, providing the context of what follows. Write about the background to your title in a way that leads naturally into the points you want to make.

Next come your **topic paragraphs**. These should be organised so that they lead your reader logically through your argument.

Finally, write your **conclusion**, which draws together the points you have already made. Don't introduce any new ideas but round off your essay with a summary that shows that you have addressed your title.

Remember:
- Use formal English: don't write like a journalist!
- Don't use abbreviations like *don't*, *can't*, *isn't*, *won't*, *it's*, *that's*.
- Avoid personal pronouns: 'We can see that building houses on flood plains can lead to flooding in heavy rain.' Instead use: 'Building houses on flood plains increases the risk of flooding in heavy rain.'
- Keep an eye on your grammar and consistency of tenses. For example, make sure that you stick to the past tense for what has happened already, especially when you are writing reports.
- Reference your work: Make sure your references in the text match up 100% with your reference list, and vice versa.

Continuing with our essay example

Here is our brainstorm: (1) Stability and stress; (2) skeletal muscle needs energy for contraction; (3) ATP as energy currency of cells; (4) glucose as energy source; (5) insulin, glucagon and pancreas; (6) blood sugar levels; (7) liver regulating glucose levels; (8) glycogen as glucose store; (9) oxidation of glucose to carbon dioxide and water; (10) lactic acid; (11) Cori cycle, carbon cycling.

Paragraph 1: Introduction: In a game of football each player runs around for a prolonged period of time and skeletal muscle is the tissue that enables this movement to happen. To function efficiently the body needs stable internal conditions, even when it is being stressed by vigorous exercise. For muscles to contract they need a readily available supply of energy in the form of ATP (adenosine triphosphate), which can be thought of as the energy currency of cells. ATP is built up using energy released from glucose through its oxidation within the muscle cells. Energy released by the breaking of chemical bonds between the atoms in glucose is trapped to make ATP and this is the energy source for contracting skeletal muscle.

Topic paragraph 2: Two hormones secreted by the pancreas regulate the amount of glucose circulating in the bloodstream. The hormones are insulin and glucagon and they have opposing effects on blood glucose levels through their actions on liver cells. Exercising muscle cells must be kept supplied with glucose. When blood glucose levels drop, the liver is stimulated by glucagon to release glucose from its carbohydrate storage molecule glycogen. The glucose molecules released from glycogen are secreted into the bloodstream, boosting the circulating levels of glucose.

Topic Paragraph 3: During vigorous exercise skeletal muscle runs short of oxygen, so it cannot fully oxidise glucose to carbon dioxide and water … ⑨ leading to a build-up of lactic acid … ⑩

Topic Paragraph 4: The liver recycles carbon from lactic acid … makes new glucose … exported into the bloodstream … restocks supplies in skeletal muscle … process called the Cori cycle. ⑪

Paragraph 5: Conclusion: pulling together the thoughts in previous paragraph …

About assessment

Assessment is the method used to grade your work against given criteria. There are two types:

1 *Formative assessment*: This work is marked and returned to you, but the grade does not count towards your assessment. The purpose is to give you an idea of how well you have done. It usually includes written feedback, giving you helpful hints on how you can improve that piece of work before final submission.

2 *Summative assessment*: This is the assessed work where the grade counts.

Assessment alphabet:

Assignment: piece of work that you are set.

Blag – don't do it!

Coursework: assessed assignment that you do unsupervised.

Deadline: final time by which you must hand work in.

Examination: formal assessment in a supervised controlled environment, usually at the end of a term or semester.

Feedback: comments on the quality of your work aimed at helping you to learn from your mistakes and improve next time.

Generic: means general, i.e., feedback that applies to most people. (Also used in the context of the common name for things, e.g., aspirin is a generic term for drugs containing acetyl salicylic acid).

The function of academic posters

The purpose of *academic conferences* is to communicate research findings and to enable networking by people working in a particular academic discipline (not just science, but any academic area).

Academic posters are often used at academic conferences where there is not sufficient time for all delegates to talk about their work. Poster sessions allow colleagues to read about your work and usually you will be present to answer questions and engage in conversations. This is sometimes called 'defending your poster' and is a skill that you will be encouraged to develop at university, along with making the poster itself.

Posters serve two functions: communication of information, and provision of a focus for a short discussion on the topic with a small number of people. It is therefore important that a poster makes a visual impact and stimulates interesting ideas for discussion. Although you may be present to defend your poster, your poster should be self-explanatory and therefore able to stand alone.

Advice on preparing posters

- Limit the amount of detail you include on a poster.
- Ensure that the print on the poster is legible from a reading distance of 1+ metres.
- Consider using diagrams, charts and pictures to illustrate your material. If you use symbols or abbreviations, it may be necessary to explain these on a 'key' in a corner of the poster.
- Make sure that your poster is easy to navigate by using unambiguous headings and a clear layout.
- Include your references at the bottom of your poster.
- Try using PowerPoint to produce your poster: work on an A4 page and have it enlarged to A1 or A0 size.
- Limit the overall text to about 300–400 words in 12pt sans serif font, e.g., Verdana and Arial, or serif, e.g., Times New Roman. This will blow up to the right size when printing your poster on A1 or A0 paper.
- Make the title 18pt and include details such as your name.

An academic poster should show evidence of:	Have I done this?
	✓
1 *Structure*	
Planning and overall organisation	
Logical format	
2 *Content*	
Clear aims	
Evidence of research	
Quality of research	
Evidence of understanding, reflection and personal insight	
Conclusions	
References	
3 *Communication*	
Communication of key points effectively	
Legibility: easy to read from approximately 1 metre distance	
Overall eye-catching presentation	

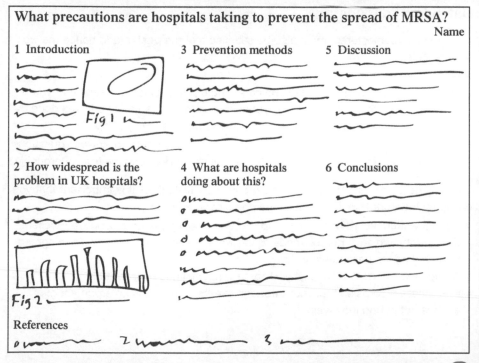

Defending your poster

At university your lecturers must also be satisfied that the poster (and hence the work it represents):

- is your own work
- does not present plagiarised or syndicated material (syndicated means that you have worked with other people without acknowledging it, so the work was done by others as well as you but you have tried to pass it off as only yours).

For these reasons you must reference your work and be able to answer questions about your poster in a way that demonstrates that you understand the topic thoroughly.

You may have been set the poster as a group-work task. If so, it is important that you divide up the work fairly between all members of your group:

- Keep a written record of all the group meetings, noting the date, who was present, the contribution each person made to the work, and what each person has agreed to do before the next meeting.
- All sign the record to show that you agree with what has been written.
- Keep these records so that your tutor can see them if there is an argument over anyone not pulling their weight.

What sort of questions can you expect?

You should expect questions requiring specific answers – the aim being to confirm that this was your own work and that you understand what you have been doing. So these may be about your methods, problems encountered in collecting your data, surprising findings from your work, suggestions for further work.

Making ends meet: paid employment
Most students in higher education need to have a paid job to help with the bills. When you get your timetable and see that you're only in classes for 8–12 hours per week you may be tempted to get a 25–30-hour-a-week job. Here's some advice: DON'T!

There is evidence that students who work in paid jobs for more than 12 hours a week do less well in their degrees than would otherwise be expected (Carter, 2006). *So … don't over-commit yourself with paid employment.*

Full-time students are expected to do about 36 hours per week of study even if their tutors are only teaching 9–12 hours of that time. That means that you need to study on your own for 24–27 hours per week. Two-thirds to three-quarters of your study is on your own, which is quite a challenge. Add in 12 hours of paid work and you have a very full week.

6 Science project work

Most final-year Honours undergraduate students and all Masters and Doctorate students will be expected to undertake some original project work. This is a substantial piece of work and is often the defining part of your degree.

Some guidelines for choosing your project

- Do pick a study that you are interested in. Read around the subject before committing yourself to a particular project.
- Talk it through with your prospective supervisor to get an idea of what is involved in terms of the type of work and the commitment expected of you.
- Make sure that your project is the right size for the timescale that you have been allocated. Be realistic and don't try to take on more than is possible in the time.

Once you have selected your project or been accepted to do a particular project, you will need to know the context of what you are trying to achieve, which is why you must carry out a full literature review, making notes.

Aims

In the light of your literature review, your next task is to work out your aims. Pose a question that is on a sensible scale and focused. Don't attempt too much. You need the right size of project for the time frame that you have available.

How to define your aims

An analogy might help you here. You are a keen mountaineer and you are planning a holiday:

1 *Topic*: Mountaineering holiday
2 *Area*: Where shall I go on holiday? You decide France
3 *Focus*: French Alps
4 *Specifics*: Chamonix district

Focusing down ...

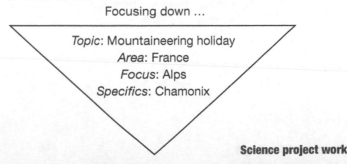

Topic: Mountaineering holiday
Area: France
Focus: Alps
Specifics: Chamonix

Here's a biological example:

1 You have chosen or been given a topic for your project: *Blood disorders*.
2 Within that topic you select *Leukaemia*.
3 Now you need to focus down into a specific research area that is of particular interest to you: *Childhood leukaemia*.
4 Next, you read specific scientific papers in that area and look out for a question that you'd like to answer: *What are the risk factors that render children vulnerable to leukaemia?*

Focusing down ...

Topic: Blood disorders
Area: Leukaemia
Focus: Childhood leukaemia
Specifics: Risk factors

Experimental design

Having read the background literature and set your aims, you must work out the pathway between the two. Planning your experimental work is key to this and you should think it through thoroughly.

Although your project is new to you, it will probably form part of ongoing research by an academic member of staff. It will have context within a research team so you need to understand this and become familiar with related work.

In designing experimental work to address the question posed in your aims you may well be required to learn new lab or field techniques. Make every effort to become competent quickly and to understand what you are doing and why. This is vital.

Writing down

Only after you have planned your work and written out your methods in your lab diary will you be ready to begin the practical work. Make sure that you keep a really good lab diary: record all your measurements, all experimental details, all outcomes even if you can't see their relevance at first.

There are no set outcomes to your project. You don't predict what will happen and try to prove it. You are doing research, so don't guess or predetermine the results.

Writing up

The format is the same as for a report so the same rules apply. The main difference is that a project is a more substantial piece of work and the methodology will have been selected by you (and your supervisor). Here is the format:

1 *Title*: Concise and precise.
2 *Abstract*: Summary – you'll write this last.
3 *Introduction*: Literature review setting the context, identifying the gaps.
4 *Aims*: Focused, concise, do-able.
5 *Materials and methods*: Accurate, complete, covering everything.
6 *Results*: Concise summary of your results in words, referring to any graphs and/or

diagrams that you have used by their appropriate figure or table number.

7 *Discussion*: Interpret your results, relate them to one another and put them into the context of your literature review. Go no further than the experiment shows. Refer back to the Aims and Introduction and discuss your results in relation to points made there. Critically assess the methods you used.

8 *Conclusions*: Summarise the whole project in a concluding page.

9 *References*: Harvard style is used in this guide and widely used in science.

10 *Appendices*: Raw data, calculations.

The road to success!

To be a successful student you need to lead a balanced life. It may help you if you start by writing the answers to these questions:

▶ Why did I decide to come to university?

▶ Why did I choose this course at this university?

▶ What do I hope to achieve in the next three years?

▶ What is my longer-term career plan?

Write this down and keep it somewhere safe so that when you find the going tough you can take it out and remind yourself of your vision for your future.

Making sense of and taking account of the feedback you are given on work you have done is a vital means by which you will learn. Comments from your tutor or lecturer on the quality of your work, often with grading, will give you an indication of the level at which you are performing.

Written feedback: You may view feedback solely in terms of the written comments that are made on your work, but during your degree, feedback will be provided in different ways that you need to recognise, all of which are designed to help you learn.

Oral feedback: This may be given during a class such as a lecture or tutorial, where the lecturer wants to tell everyone present about issues with the work that apply generally (generic feedback). For example: there may have been a common error in calculations from a piece of fieldwork, so rather than correct each person's calculations, the lecturer may choose to do the calculation in class for everybody to see. This also offers the opportunity for questions about the calculation method, etc.

Peer feedback: Here other students are your peers, so this is student-to-student feedback usually given by you or to you orally or using a structured 'check list'.

Written feedback

This is the most common form of feedback and more easily recognised by students.

Imagine you have just had the draft of an essay returned to you with written feedback. *Question*: What are you going to do with it? You have various options:

1 Ignore the comments completely and submit your essay as it is.

2 Read the comments, screw up your nose, complain in your head or out loud and put the work aside. Later you make a few minor adjustments (not paying attention to the feedback) and submit the essay in almost the same form as before.

3 Read the comments, maybe still screw up your nose and complain in your head or out loud, then sit down and work through the comments in a constructive way.

If you want to respond as in option 3 but are not sure where to begin, then here are guidelines on how to do it.

Learning cycle

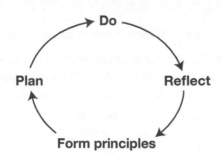

Do: Identify characteristics of your work. What do you notice about your work? What does it look like? What mistakes do you make? What is good about it?

Reflect: A tutor's comments are usually designed to draw your attention to how you write or think and to enable you to see things – good and bad – that you may not otherwise have seen. Use these comments to prompt your own reflection. So ... tutor notes X. What do you think they are trying to tell you and what are your own observations?

Form principles: What do you need to work on? If you are to change and not simply repeat the same pattern of errors, what do you need to target?

Plan: OK – so what are you going to *do* about it? Get as specific as possible. This is an ACTION PLAN.

You might find it helpful to use this table to work through your coursework feedback:

Do: Identify characteristics of your work.	Reflect: Tutor's comments: what do you understand by this? Your observations.	Form principles: What do you need to work on (personal objectives)?	Plan: Action plan: What are you going to do about it?

Source: Reproduced by kind permission of Kate Williams.

Exam preparation

Revision = Re-vision = seeing again: assumes that you have already made good notes from your lectures and reading. Revision is not starting from scratch with your study.

Assuming that you did do the work during the teaching period, you will have comprehensive notes for each of your subjects. If not, you will need to do a damage limitation exercise: make sure you have notes from all of your lectures. For any missing topics you will need to make notes from your textbook.

Planning your revision

- *Make a weekly timetable*, taking into account fixed points such as revision tutorials, paid employment and other commitments.
- *Each day, allocate blocks of time* when you will be revising, interspersed with blocks of time that you will use for relaxation. A block of time may be a morning, afternoon or evening. You may need to plan in time when you will be doing your paid job, looking after family, too.

- *Plan out a topic for each study block*, covering all the material that you need to revise, and bearing in mind your exam timetable. Don't try to revise one subject for days on end – to maintain your interest, vary your subjects during each day.
- *Divide up each block into bite-sized chunks*. Don't attempt to study for 3 hours without a break. Have a go at 30–40 minutes, then a 10-minute break, followed by another 30–40 minute study session. That way you won't become over-tired or bored.
- *Allocate study topics to study times*. You may prefer to stick with one subject for a day, but allocate your bite-sized chunks of time to different topics within one subject. Or you may prefer to vary your subjects more frequently. Much depends on how easy you find it to stay interested and motivated.

How to do your revision

Use a variety of approaches. Here are a few ideas:

▶ You will probably need to start by reading your lecture notes, then refer to your textbook to clear up any uncertainties.

▶ Take this opportunity to read further on topics covered in your lectures. You will gain extra marks in your exam if there is evidence that you have read beyond the material covered in your lectures.

▶ Most textbooks have questions at the end of each chapter. Have a go at answering them. Then look back in your book and read through the relevant section again to see how well you got on.

▶ Look out for online revision questions on the websites for your textbooks.

Types of exam

University science exams take a number of forms: multiple choice questions, short answer questions and essay questions.

1 Multiple choice question papers (MCQs)

▸ Often used to assess first-year work where the objective is to see how much information you know and have understood.

▸ May sound like an easy option, but they require you to have precise knowledge since the choices of options given you may all be correct to a certain extent.

▸ You are required to be discriminating and to choose the one that most accurately answers the question.

▸ MCQs can take the form of *calculation papers* that will require you to calculate the answer before choosing.

▸ The options you will be given are likely to include the most common calculation errors encountered by staff – so beware: do the calculation and don't guess!

For example:

Question	Select one answer	Tick one box
You have 1L of buffer at pH 8.6. What volume of phosphoric acid do you need to add to bring it to pH 7.4? (molarity of H_3PO_3 is....	A *Correct units of volume but decimal point in the wrong place so answer incorrect*	A
	B *Answer has incorrect units of volume but numerically correct*	B
	C *Numerically correct answer with correct units of volume*	C ✓
	D *Incorrect calculation and units*	D

▸ MCQ papers often have some form of negative marking to discourage you from guessing. Typically a wrong answer may attract a penalty of -0.25 of a mark.

Useful strategy for MCQs: Work out how many minutes you have for each question (e.g., 60 questions in 90 minutes gives you 1.5 minutes per question). Go through all the questions, answering those you can do and leaving those you can't do easily. After attempting all questions, go back to the more difficult ones. Watch the clock as you will be under time pressure.

2 Short answer questions

▶ These require *you* to have the ideas, the correct terms, etc.
▶ Look at the marking scheme. If a question is worth a considerable proportion of the marks then it will require more than one simple idea.
▶ Mostly you will not be required to regurgitate facts but interpret the question in the light of your knowledge.

Useful strategy for short questions: Work out the allocation of marks. Here is a table showing the time allocation per question for questions carrying equal marks:

Length of exam	Number of questions	Time per question (minutes)
1 hour (60 mins)	2 3 4	30 20 15
2 hours (120 mins)	2 3 4	60 40 30
2.5 hours (150 mins)	2 3 4 5	75 50 35–40 30

For papers with unequally weighted sections then you need to work out your timings carefully. For example, for papers with Section A = one essay worth 50% and Section B = short questions worth 50%:

Length of exam	Section A (50%): Time (mins)	Section B (50%)	
		No. of questions	Time per question (mins)
1 hour (60 mins)	30	2 3	15 10
2 hours (120 mins)	60	2 3 4	30 20 15

3 Essay questions

▶ Use the same format as described in the essay section.
▶ Main difference: you probably won't be able to specify your sources, though if you can name the key players in the area of science that you are describing, you will be given credit for these.

Exam time management

One of the most important factors when sitting your exam is managing your time well. You need to plan your exam time, recognising the type of paper, number of questions, proportioning of marks.

The most tricky exams to manage are those with essay questions. Try this:

▶ *Read the paper carefully*, noting what choice you have – how many questions you must answer, etc.

▶ *Think* what each question is asking.

▶ *Attempt the correct number of questions*. If you are required to answer four questions, attempting only three means that you will only be marked out of 75%; attempting two questions on a three-question paper lowers your maximum mark to 66%.

▶ *Questions involving calculations* may look daunting at first, but it is easier to get high marks on these questions compared with straight essay questions. The key here is to show all your working out. You will be given credit for using the correct method even if you slip up on the number crunching. If you only give an answer without workings, you'll get one mark for a correct answer and nothing if you get it wrong.

Timekeeping: Divide the exam time up between the questions according to the marks weighting. If you have a 2-hour exam with three questions carrying equal marks, then you should spend about 35–40 minutes on each. Use 5–7 minutes to plan your answer, write for 30 minutes, then spend 2–3 minutes reading through what you have written.

Plan your essay: Take 5–7 minutes to draw up your plan. *Brainstorm* everything you can recall relating to the question until you have no more ideas; *number the ideas* in a logical order ready to answer that question.

Now write it! Because you have planned your essay you will find that you are thinking about what you are writing, rather than worrying about what will come next – that is sorted because you have already organised your ideas.

And remember – don't write 'everything you know about something'. Exam questions are specific and require specific answers. It is unlikely to be appropriate that you regurgitate word for word something that you have read. You will have to work your knowledge into a suitable answer for the specific question that has been asked.

Description **Here's an example of an exam essay question:** — 2 part question

What are the challenges faced by organisms that live on the tidal seashore and how are they adapted to meet these challenges? Illustrate your answer with reference to one named plant or alga and one named animal.

specific examples — specific examples

Brainstorm: *Challenges*: wet then dry due to tides, salt water, wind, desiccation by the sun, evaporation leading to more salty conditions, hostile environment (explain) … *Adaptations*: excrete salt, thick cuticle, high internal salt levels, clamp down on the rock when exposed to the air, combat osmotic stresses, … *Examples*: *Fucus vesiculosus* (bladder-wrack seaweed) and mollusc *Diodora apertura* (keyhole limpet).

Number the ideas: *Challenges*: (1) hostile environment; (2) salt water; (3) wet then dry due to tides; (4) desiccation by the sun and wind; (5) evaporation leading to more salty conditions … *Adaptations*: (1) combat osmotic stresses; (2) thick cuticle; (3) high internal salt levels; (4) excrete salt; (5) clamp down on the rock when exposed to the air … *Examples*: *Fucus vesiculosus* (bladder-wrack seaweed) and mollusc *Diodora apertura* (keyhole limpet).

Keep an eye on the clock because …

Figure 5 shows you the efficiency of gaining marks as you write your essay. Here you have 40 minutes to answer a question; 5–7 minutes are reading and planning time so you have *30–35 minutes for writing your essay.*

▸ Note that the graph is not linear.
▸ You rapidly gain marks during the first half hour; then your productivity drops off.
▸ If you carry on writing beyond the allotted 30–35 minutes then you pick up very few extra marks but you eat into the time allocated for another question.

The **take-away message** is that it is false economy to spend longer than the allotted time on one question at the expense of another question. By all means go back to an earlier question after you have attempted the right number of questions in your exam, but *do not spend longer on an early question at the expense of your final one.*

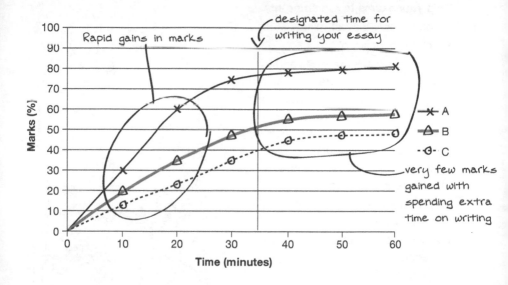

Figure 5: How A, B and C grade students gain marks while answering an exam question allocated 30–35 minutes, and how spending longer on a question is not efficient in terms of extra marks gained.

Help your exams to run smoothly

- Don't overdo the last-minute study.
- Get plenty of sleep!
- Make sure you know when and where your exams take place.
- Check that you have the equipment you need (pens, pencils, eraser, sharpener, ruler, calculator if allowed) in a clear colourless bag.
- Plan your journey, bearing in mind traffic congestion etc.
- Arrive at the exam room with time to spare (20+ minutes).
- Follow the invigilator's instructions exactly.

Final comment

So there you have it – a brief guide to studying science covering some of the basic skills that scientists use. I hope that you will be excited by studying science: exploring the natural world, the diversity of life and the reasoning behind it. Read widely, be open-minded, embrace new ideas, have a go at problem solving, do science. Above all, be prepared to continue learning throughout your life, because the more you know, the more you'll realise that there is to learn!

References

Carter, C (2006) 'Expectation versus reality: how do first year students allocate their time?' Proceedings of the 1st EFYE conference, University of Teesside.

Godwin, J (2009) *Planning Your Essay*. Basingstoke: Palgrave Macmillan.

Robbins, SK (2007) PASS staff and student help sheets (unpublished).

Williams, K and Carroll, J (2009) *Referencing and Understanding Plagiarism*. Basingstoke: Palgrave Macmillan.

Science jargon used in this book

Absorbance Reading from a spectrophotometer (has no units) relating to how much of a substance you have in your solution.

Pipette Graduated instrument used to transfer exact volumes of liquid.

Pipetting Act of using a pipette to transfer liquid.

Precipitate Matter that solidifies and drops to the bottom of the container usually as the result of a chemical reaction.

Proportional relationship The amount of one thing is linked directly to another thing so that when you change one, the other changes automatically too.

Replicates When you have two or more copies of something, e.g., you make up three identical samples for an experiment to test whether the result is consistent.

Solubility Describes how well a substance dissolves, usually in a liquid such as water.

Solution (chemical term) A mixture that results when you dissolve one substance (e.g., solid, gas or liquid) in another, usually liquid so that it all looks the same. Process can be reversed.

Spectrophotometer Electronic instrument that uses light of a single wavelength to measure the concentration of a solution by recording how much of the light is absorbed by the sample (absorbance).

Treatments The different things that you do to your samples to test what happens. You have a control with which to compare your treatments.

Index